Original title:
Island Reflections

Copyright © 2025 Creative Arts Management OÜ
All rights reserved.

Author: Ethan Prescott
ISBN HARDBACK: 978-1-80581-557-0
ISBN PAPERBACK: 978-1-80581-084-1
ISBN EBOOK: 978-1-80581-557-0

Serenity Wrapped in Layers of Blue

The waves waltz in a quirky dance,
While crabs take their misfit chance.
Sandcastles built, but oh so meek,
A royal shanty, just a peek!

Seagulls squawk their silly calls,
Trying to sell clam shells at mall stalls.
A beach ball bounces, flies askew,
And sunburned noses turn a hue!

In flip-flops worn, we stroll with glee,
Tripping on towels, lost in spree.
Beach drinks spill—a fruity blast,
We laugh at mishaps, none are cast.

As sunset paints with shades of fun,
We toast to laughter, our day's begun.
With friends so dear, we share a cheer,
Wrapped in joy, with nothing to fear!

Beneath the Banyan's Watch

Beneath the banyan's mighty sway,
The locals laugh and dance all day.
A monkey steals the coconut feast,
As we all cheer for our little beast.

The roots twist like a grandma's yarn,
With tales of mischief that we soarn.
A parrot drops a wordy joke,
And in the shade we share and poke.

A Canvas of Blue Reflections

The sea's a painting, bright and bold,
With waves that dance and stories told.
We squint at fishes in a line,
Who swim away as if to dine.

A painted sky, a screeching gull,
While crabs play tag, their shells a hull.
We splash and giggle in the sun,
Each moment here is laughter's run.

Fish Tales Beneath the Surface

Beneath the waves, fish plot their scheme,
With scales that shimmer, they hardly gleam.
They gossip over seaweed beds,
And laugh at all the rumors fed.

A fish with glasses claims he's wise,
Says he can teach the stars to rise.
But when a shark swims close for lunch,
The wise fish hides—he packs a punch!

Where Time Pauses to Breathe

Where time stands still and giggles sprout,
We boast of tales, there's never doubt.
With seashells worn as crowns of pride,
We rule this realm with fun as guide.

The sun sets down, a golden ball,
While crickets chirp, we hear their call.
Laughter lingers in the night,
As fireflies twinkle, pure delight.

Seagulls Above

Seagulls squawk, they steal my fries,
Bald heads atop with eager eyes.
They dive and swoop, a clumsy dance,
While I just sit, caught in a trance.

Fried crumbs rain down like confetti bright,
The birds rejoice in their silly flight.
They cackle loud, they mock my plight,
As I wave back, feeling light.

Shadows Below

In the water, my shadow dives,
As fish swim by, they play high-fives.
I wave my hands, they laugh away,
With tails that flick, they skedaddle and sway.

My shadow's here, the real one's gone,
Gone to get coffee, I'm left to fawn.
I chat with fish, they call me 'mate',
While my shadow flirts with a crusty crate.

Waters of Introspection

Looking down at the water's face,
My thoughts drift round in a splashy race.
A rubber duck holds philosophic chat,
While I ponder life, trapped under a hat.

Waves carry dreams to another shore,
As I weigh my woes with a jelly core.
The sea gives laughs, it knows my plight,
While the rubber duck just keeps it light.

Sublime Horizons and Lost Suns

The horizon waves with a cheeky grin,
A radiant sun dips, ready to spin.
I chase my thoughts, as colors blend,
But my ice cream cone drops; that's the end.

As shadows stretch and giggles fade,
I trip and stumble—who needs to wade?
Lost suns beam down with mischievous glee,
As I cartwheel home, slightly less free.

Alchemy of the Sea Breeze

The sea breeze whispers a cheeky tune,
Teasing my hair like a mischievous raccoon.
With every gust, my hat takes flight,
I chase it down, what a silly sight!

It dances high, then dips in low,
The wind is laughing, putting on a show.
While salt and laughter blend with ease,
The alchemy's wild, brought forth by the breeze.

Palms Swaying in Silence

The palms are dancing, oh so high,
Like they've heard a really funny lie.
Leaves whisper secrets, wild and true,
"Have you seen my hat? I lost it too!"

The crabs tiptoe, all dressed in red,
Making quick plans while avoiding bread.
Seagulls squawk, their gossip flows,
"Who stole my fries? Now everyone knows!"

Stories Held by the Wind

The wind carries tales from the sea,
Of a fish who tried to climb a tree.
He flopped and floundered, what a sight,
Said, "I just wanted to soar in flight!"

A parrot squawks, "That's quite the yarn!"
"You think that's wild? Just wait till dawn!"
A dolphin grins, "I'll join the fun!"
"Let's race to the clouds, oh what a run!"

Beneath the Azure Veil

Beneath the blue, a fish does prance,
In a weird little underwater dance.
A starfish snickers, "Look at him go!"
"His moves are so bad, he'll steal the show!"

An octopus waves with eight long limbs,
Says, "Join my band for oceanic hymns!"
But they all swim off, a swift retreat,
Not ready to groove to squishy beats!

Nirvana of the Coral Reef

Corals giggle in dazzling hues,
Holding a party, spreading the blues.
"A clownfish named Bob has lost his way,
He swam in circles, all night and day!"

The turtles roll, they can't keep still,
Trying to chase the sun for a thrill.
"Do you think we'll catch it? What a feat!"
"Only if we pick up speed on our feet!"

Secrets Beneath the Palm

Underneath the swaying fronds,
Lies a treasure, made of ponds.
Frogs in sunglasses croak with style,
Winking at the waves all the while.

Crabs in mittens dance around,
Juggling shells upon the ground.
Seagulls now play peek-a-boo,
Taking bets on who flies through.

Lemonade spills from the tree,
As chattering monkeys hold a spree.
With giggles echoing on the shore,
As fish watch the shenanigans galore.

So let's cheers to the palm's grand show,
With laughter that's set to overflow!
What secrets does it guard, I ask?
Perhaps it's just good humor's task!

Symphony of the Salt Breeze

The salt breeze sings a silly tune,
With sandcastles built very strewn.
A hermit crab plays guitar so loud,
Making waves join its music proud.

Flip-flops flapping left and right,
A dance party steals the night.
Dolphins leap, quite debonair,
Chasing rainbows in salty air.

Kites flutter overhead with glee,
While snails slide on a water spree.
Mermaids giggle, toss a friend,
In this fun, we'll never end.

So come and join this jolly jest,
Where salt and laughter are the best.
We'll sway to nature's quirky cue,
In this symphony, just me and you!

Twilight's Embrace

As twilight wraps the sun's lost glow,
Crickets join the wave's soft flow.
Fireflies blink in silly fun,
While fish perform under the sun.

Under the stars, a hammock sways,
With coconuts spinning in their plays.
Laughter echoes from the shore,
As jellyfish dance forevermore.

Turtles play hide and seek in sand,
While starfish clap, a beachy band.
With giggles rolling like the tide,
We bask in joy, our hearts are wide.

Twilight whispers with a grin,
Pulling all the joy within.
With funny tales we weave and trace,
Sunset charms our funny place.

Fragments of a Coastal Memory

A seagull's hat flies through the air,
As someone's sandwich goes with flair.
Turtles gossip in the sun,
Sharing tales of silly run.

Shells are stacked in goofy rows,
With more stories than one quite knows.
Waves whisper jokes to the sandy floor,
As crab slippers dance out by the shore.

A picnic blanket flips and rolls,
As laughter fills up all the holes.
With marshmallows toast on the fire's dance,
While tiny fish join in the prance.

These fragments float, each laugh we keep,
In ocean's heart, the joys so deep.
With every wave and every jest,
Coastal memories are surely blessed!

The Stillness Between Storms

Clouds rumble like a hungry beast,
The calm feels like a borrowed feast.
Seagulls dance with silly grace,
While the sea murmurs in a soft embrace.

Waves whisper jokes too deep for land,
As crabs shuffle about, oh so unplanned.
A ship captain dons a pirate hat,
Singing sea shanties and chasing his cat.

Shells gather secrets from the deep,
Fish play tag, making mermaids leap.
The wind tells stories of mariners bold,
Who'd trade their treasure for tales retold.

Then comes the storm, all laughter flies,
As umbrellas dance 'neath darkened skies.
But once it's over, what a show!
The wind still chuckles at the waves' low blow.

Tide Pools of Introspection

Gazing down at the water's eye,
Where tiny worlds of wonders lie.
A starfish waves with a lazy cheer,
While a jellyfish jigs with no fear.

Crabs wear hats made of seaweed strands,
As a snail sails on the wet, warm sands.
A little fish shakes its slippery head,
"Stay out of trouble, or you'll end up dead!"

Meandering thoughts join the tide's play,
Worrying if they'll drown someday.
Peering deep into watery wells,
Finding life's secrets in gentle swells.

The tide pulls back, just like time,
Leaving behind a salty rhyme.
With each splash, they laugh and sigh,
What's deeper than water? Just give it a try!

Driftwood Conversations

A log lounges, worn and wise,
Telling tales of storms and skies.
"Once I was a towering tree,
Now I'm a bench for you and me!"

Two barnacles nod with a grin,
"We hitch a ride and scratch your skin!
Popped up here just to make noise,
Who knew driftwood had such poise?"

A soda can chimes in, full of sass,
"Thought I could float, but man, I'm brass!
I'm just here for the party scenes,
Rusty and rough, faded jeans."

The tide ebbs low, but laughter's high,
As the sun sets like a big, bold pie.
Driftwood's wise, though a little absurd,
For every wave, there's a laugh unheard.

Twilight Musings by the Sea

As the sun dips, the stars prepare,
The moon winks down, with a halcyon stare.
Crabs whisper secrets, cheeky and spry,
While jellyfish float, "Oh my, oh my!"

Fishermen dream of monster fish tales,
While mermaids exchange their glittering scales.
A dolphin jumps, the ocean's delight,
Making us giggle in fading light.

Cool breezes weave through tousled hair,
Tickling noses, bringing laughter to air.
Seashells chuckle, collecting night's sound,
As beach towels shuffle within joyful bounds.

Twilight wraps the world in a hug,
While sandcastles snooze, circled snug.
With each wave that whispers to me,
I ponder highs and the silliness of the sea.

Uncharted Waters Within

In a sea of socks, I dive deep,
Finding treasures I'll never keep.
A rubber duck floats by my side,
In this ocean, I cannot hide.

With each wave comes a silly grin,
As fishy tales begin to spin.
A mermaid laughs with hair so wild,
'These silly currents make me a child!'

I bring my snorkel, but where's the fish?
Only bubbles grant my every wish.
A pirate's hat upon my head,
'This ship's a toy, but I feel dread!'

So grab a surfboard made of dreams,
Ride these tides of whimsy streams.
Laughter echoes through the spray,
Uncharted waters, come what may!

Luminescence of Twilight

Stars blink like tipsy fireflies,
Wobbling through the purple skies.
The moon wears shades, thinks it's so cool,
While crickets chirp their nightly school.

A coconut drops, but not a snack,
A brilliant glow brings the night back.
'That light's a sign,' a seagull squawks,
'Time for catch-up in funny talks!'

The ocean glimmers, but not with gold,
Just shellfish gossip making us bold.
Tidal waves of laughter rise,
As night dances in playful guise.

So gather 'round as shadows play,
Awkward poses in fine ballet.
With each chuckle, the stars align,
In this absurd and twinkling shrine!

Portraits in Sand

I sculpt a castle with grand flair,
Only to find it's just a chair.
A lobster nods in approval so grand,
While I reach for snacks, not a strand!

With buckets bright and shovels new,
I make a moat—who knew it grew?
The tide comes in, it steals my pride,
My sandy stockpile takes a ride.

Footprints tell stories of silly fun,
A crab does the moonwalk, on the run.
I ask for wisdom from a clam,
"Tell me, wise one, what is my jam?"

The seagulls caw in a playful jest,
'The beach is your canvas, now do your best!'
As waves come crashing, my dreams expand,
Creating portraits all in sand!

Chasing Misty Sunsets

The sun dons shades, it's quite the sight,
As clouds puff cotton, in evening light.
I chase the glow, with giggles near,
'This sunset's mine, just don't you steer!'

My shadow dances with every stride,
Tripping on air, a playful guide.
With laughter bubbling like bright champagne,
I'm never running, just feigning pain.

The horizon blushes, I give a wink,
'This chase is serious, don't you think?'
But then a dolphin leaps, and I stop dead,
'Wait up, my sunset!' I jokingly said.

So I'll gather colors, put them on toast,
A breakfast feast of the things I boast.
With skies on fire and hearts alight,
Chasing sunbeams through the night!

Voices of the Wind and Waves

Whispers of the breeze come play,
Tickling my ears in a cheeky way.
The waves giggle as they crash,
Making my worries vanish in a splash.

Seagulls squawk in a raucous choir,
Plucking my heartstrings with their desire.
Each laugh echoes from sea to shore,
Nature's jesters, can't help but adore.

Sand castles rise, then tumble down,
A royal decree from the sandy crown.
My pail is a vessel of dreams and grins,
As laughter dances on sun-kissed fins.

Bubble-blowing waves weave their tale,
A slippery tale that can never fail.
With each tide that comes, I spark and gleam,
In this merry banquet, life feels like a dream.

A Symphony in Blue

In the dance of boats, I'm swaying too,
Listening to the tunes of the ocean's brew.
Fish flit by with a comedic flair,
While the sun composes with mucky hair.

Waves conspire like giggling friends,
Nudging each other as their energy bends.
The sky feels heavy with laughter's tune,
Where clouds wear hats and the sun's a cartoon.

Seashells chuckle as they play on the sand,
Singing sweet songs with their lotioned hand.
A conch shell whispers, "Come join our fun!"
While starfish throw shade under the sun.

As I twirl with the breeze like a child at play,
I marvel at how humor helps keep gloom at bay.
Each splash and giggle holds life's finest view,
Creating a symphony painted in blue.

Secrets of the Sunset Shore

The sun slips down in a silly show,
Painting the waves in a fiery glow.
Shells gossip softly about the day,
While crabs scuttle with much to say.

Laughter erupts from the beach's edge,
As families gather near a makeshift hedge.
Between shouts and splashes the stories unfold,
Each secret shimmer, a treasure to hold.

The horizon wears colors both peculiar and bright,
While dogs chase seagulls, an ongoing plight.
The breeze tickles cheeks, soft as a sigh,
As it carries the whispers of the tide's lullaby.

Moments of joy held tightly in hand,
All woven together in this golden land.
As the sun takes a bow, I laugh and adore,
These hilarious secrets of the evening shore.

Grains of Time Between my Toes

Each grain of sand, a secret resides,
Tickling my feet as it playfully slides.
With each wiggled toe, I hear giggles galore,
A chorus of laughter from the ocean's roar.

Time stands still as the tides play tricks,
Shells count the seconds with their salty clicks.
I'm a mere jester in this sandy throne,
Beneath a sky where silly clouds have grown.

Jumping waves play tag, they splash with glee,
While flip-flops abandon me, wild and free.
Laughter erupts with each slip and flop,
As the sun's rays cheer me, "Don't ever stop!"

Grains of time spill like candy from jars,
As I chase my dreams 'neath the squeaky stars.
Each moment a giggle, a dance in the light,
In this sandy wonder where joy feels just right.

Ebb and Flow of Forgotten Tales

Once I found a crab so wise,
He wore a hat and told me lies.
He claimed to surf on waves of cream,
And danced like fish in a silly dream.

A seagull stole my sandwich slice,
He squawked, 'This is my paradise!'
I chased him 'round the sandy shore,
But he just laughed and asked for more.

The tides came in with giggles loud,
As shells formed letters in the crowd.
They spelled my name, then washed away,
A prankster's note to start the day.

So here I sit by bubbling brine,
With tales of crabs and birds divine.
In puddles deep, I dip my toes,
And wonder where the laughter goes.

Coastal Reverie at Sunrise

The sun popped up, a yolk so bright,
But birds were up, ready to fight.
They squawked and swooped, a morning race,
As I just yawned, lost in my space.

A fish jumped high, as if to say,
'Come on now, join the splashy play!'
I tried my best to start a swim,
But belly-flopped, and made a din.

The waves rolled in rehearsed ballet,
While seaweed twirled in grand display.
With starfish winking in delight,
I giggled hard at such a sight.

As footprints faded in the sand,
I drew a heart with clumsy hand.
Sunrise whispers filled the air,
'Join the fun, don't fret or stare!'

As the Waves Whisper Secrets

The tide came in with gossip fresh,
Tales of sandcastles, all enmesh.
A clam snickered, 'Did you see?
They turned to puddles, how funny!'

The seafoam giggled, tickled toes,
While jellyfish danced in fancy clothes.
I tried to join, but tripped and fell,
They laughed so hard, I rang a bell.

A seashell whispered, 'Can you hear?
Mermaids swim with lots of cheer!'
But when I turned to take a peek,
They hid away, too shy to speak.

Each wave that rolled brought new surprise,
With ocean secrets, oh so wise.
In salty air, I felt quite free,
As laughter echoed by the sea.

Mirage of the Sunlit Pool

In the pool I saw a fish in shades,
Wearing sunglasses, throwing parades.
He splashed around in a dance so bold,
Claiming he had treasures untold.

A beach ball bounced, and so did I,
We laughed and rolled beneath the sky.
While turtles raced in slow-motion style,
I cheered them on with a silly smile.

The sun was hot, a golden flare,
But my lazy float was like a chair.
I dreamed of waves while sipping tea,
With a rubber duck right next to me.

The mirage shimmered with magic fun,
As shadows danced, and time would run.
In every splash and every grin,
I found my joy, let the laughter in.

Celestial Serenade on the Breeze

Stars above twinkle and dance,
While crabs clumsily steal a glance.
The moon plays tricks on the waves,
As fish plan their cheeky escapades.

Seagulls squawk jokes with delight,
While the sandcastles reach new height.
A beach ball rolls out of control,
Chasing kids through surf and stroll.

Laughter echoes through the night,
As waves crash with all their might.
A jellyfish does a little jig,
While dolphins giggle, feeling big.

Underneath this cosmic sheen,
We dance like no one's ever seen.
With all the quirks the ocean shares,
Seaweed wigs and salty flairs.

The Lure of Forgotten Beaches

Once I found a flip-flop lone,
Suntanned and sad, it made me groan.
A starfish waved from the deep,
While seagulls plotted their cheeky sweep.

Old driftwood laughed at its peers,
Telling tales of forgotten years.
A coconut rolled down the shore,
And a crab said, 'I've seen that before!'

Sand castles built with great care,
Were wrecked by the toddler's affair.
Shells whispered secrets, a fun little scheme,
While the tide played a prank on the dream.

The sun set low with a wink,
While seaweed danced in a sync.
That beach held memories anew,
Where laughter was the ocean's brew.

Reflections on Sheltered Sands

In secluded corners where giggles rise,
We find buried treasures, much to our surprise.
A sea turtle joins in the fun,
Wearing sunglasses, ready to run.

Shells hum tunes that make us grin,
While sandy feet do a little spin.
A jelly bean washed up with the tide,
Declared itself the beach's pride.

Funky shells in a vibrant hue,
Play peekaboo amidst the blue.
The ocean's a riddle, silly and sweet,
A place where laughter never meets defeat.

With blankets spread for picnics galore,
And seagulls eyeing every morsel I store.
The sunset competes with colors so bold,
Painting memories, worthy of gold.

Solitary Lanterns at Twilight

Lanterns flicker, casting a glow,
As crickets sing their evening show.
A lone fish splashes, quite the brawl,
   As if to say, 'Catch me, if at all!'

Mysterious waves tell secrets untold,
While shadows of palm trees grow bold.
A flamingo wobbles, tries to dance,
Who knew such long legs needed a chance?

Snacking on seaweed, it's quite the treat,
While hermit crabs shuffle on tiny feet.
The twilight embraces all silly glee,
As the moon giggles in a mischievous spree.

With the ocean's laughter wrapped 'round our waist,
We recall the moments that cannot be chased.
A hilarious soirée beneath starlit skies,
Where every twinkle is a funny surprise.

The Whispering Current

In the creek where gossip flows,
Fish wear hats and dance in rows.
Turtles chuckle, passing by,
Splashing frogs that leap and fly.

A crab in a vest, so proud and spry,
Claims the throne beneath the sky.
Every wave, a secret shared,
With giggles that the shoreline dared.

Seagulls squawk, like old pals tease,
Juggling shells on the gentle breeze.
The current whispers, 'Dive right in!'
With a wink, we know we'll win.

In this watery realm of fun and play,
Where laughter rolls, come what may.
We'll ride the ripples, take the dare,
Life's a splash—join us if you dare!

Mirrored Dreams on the Water's Edge

Reflections smile, oh what a sight,
Fish in suits twirl left and right.
The sun winks off the surface bright,
As mermaids giggle, quite the delight.

Clouds play coy, like silly friends,
Casting shadows that twist and bend.
A hammock strung between two trees,
Bounces gently, sways with ease.

Water smiles with each plop and splash,
While frogs compete in a silly dash.
With goofy grins, we take a seat,
Nature's silliness can't be beat.

Under this sky of whims and cheer,
We'll dance with waves, there's nothing to fear.
Join the fun at the water's edge,
Where dreams are spun, right on the ledge!

Patterns in the Sand

Footprints dig in, a comic trail,
Waves chase backs, never fail.
Sandcastles rise with might,
Only to crumble by night.

Seashells are treasures, they say,
But one just cracked and ran away!
Laughter echoes in every grain,
Creating patterns that conceal pain.

A crab wearing shades strolls the beach,
While kids listen, with tales to teach.
Seagull serenades, a funny tune,
As the sun bows down, embracing the moon.

Our beachside giggles blend with the breeze,
Like joyous whispers in the trees.
In patterns drawn by a playful hand,
Life's just silly in the warm, soft sand!

Lost in the Lullaby of Waves

The waves hum softly, a playful song,
While starfish ponder where they belong.
Clams clap shells, keeping the beat,
As seaweed dances, swaying sweet.

Bubbles rise, like thoughts in our heads,
Tickling toes while laughter spreads.
Seashells giggle, each one a friend,
In this aquatic realm where fun won't end.

Tides tease the shore, pulling us near,
As jellyfish float, spreading good cheer.
The moon joins in with a wink and a grin,
What a ride when you dive right in!

In this lullaby sung by the sea,
We lose ourselves completely, oh so free.
Every splash tells a tale to embrace,
It's a frolicsome dance, a water-bound chase!

Beyond the Breaking Tide

The waves crash down with a laugh,
A crab scuttles fast, splits in half.
Seagulls squawk in high-pitched glee,
Chasing fish as they dart and flee.

Sunburnt tourists, red as a flame,
Lost their shades, but snatched a game.
Watermelons float, a silly sight,
A picnic party that took flight.

Buckets of sand, castles with flair,
But the tide comes in, without a care.
Surfboards wipe out, splashes abound,
As laughter erupts all around.

Life's a beach, oh what a hoot,
Flip-flops flying, a runaway boot.
With every splash and every smile,
We'll celebrate life's wacky style.

Shadows Dancing in the Surf

Footprints in sand, a comic trail,
Chasing shadows, we set sail.
Riptides pulling, we squeal with fright,
But dolphins jump in pure delight.

Umbrellas flip, a carnival sight,
Windswept hair, and sunburned bite.
A seagull swoops for a snack to munch,
Grabbing a chip from our beachy lunch.

Kites soaring high, a colorful cheer,
Kids running wild, with grit and gear.
Sandcastles tumble, oh what a mess,
But laughter embraces the sandy stress.

Waves crash down in a playful jest,
Bringing a soggy, sun-soaked quest.
From sunrise fun to sunset's glow,
We dance in shadows, the tide's soft flow.

Nautical Musings

Stowed away on a boat so small,
The captain sneezes, we rock and sprawl.
Sea cucumbers, the oddest of sights,
Giggling fish in their flippery flights.

A fishing pole bows, what's on the line?
A boot, a sock – oh, how divine!
Shouting at bubbles, the sea so vast,
Here's hoping the laughs forever last.

The compass spins, oh what a tease,
Lost in waves or sipping teas?
Nautical charts turn into doodles,
Our knowledge sinking with old noodles.

Together we find, in salt and spray,
The humor in every twisty way.
With laughter echoing, we roam the sea,
Where joy and silliness are truly free.

Lighthouses of the Heart

Guiding light on a wobbly beam,
This beacon knows just how to beam.
Mismatched socks on the rocky shore,
With every wave, it begs for more.

Fishermen laugh at their tangled lines,
With worms that wiggle like silly vines.
A lighthouse keeper dances in glee,
To the octopus's polka spree.

Each flicker shines with a goofy glow,
Chasing sunsets that steal the show.
A beacon of jokes in the night's embrace,
Waving goodnight with a fishy face.

Oh, the fun that the sea imparts,
With laughter chiming in our hearts.
A lighthouse stands where wild waves play,
Bringing joy to the end of the day.

Rhythms of the Ocean's Heart

The waves dance like they're at a ball,
Splashing water onto all who call.
Seagulls gossip, squawking with glee,
While fish underneath just want to flee.

The tide comes in, and my hair does too,
A salty comb-over, oh what a view!
Crabs march sideways, a quirky parade,
Making sure their big plans won't be delayed.

Sunbathers bake like bread in the sun,
As toddlers run wild, just wanting to run.
Caught in a game of splash and retreat,
Life's a beach until you lose your seat.

As sunset paints the world in bright hues,
We laugh at the sand stuck in our shoes.
In the ocean's embrace, we find our part,
Swaying along to the rhythm of the heart.

Waters like Glass

The sea is calm, like a mirror bright,
Reflecting clouds in a comical light.
Fish wear shades, lounging as they please,
While turtles sunbathe, swaying like trees.

Children skip stones, aiming for dreams,
Each splash a giggle, laughter it seems.
Weep like the ocean? No, just a drip!
As time floats away on a jellyfish trip.

A squirrel swims, surprising the crew,
Waving its tail like it's trying to woo.
Drifting boats nod, with sails on their heads,
The pirates are now just sipping cold spreads.

As moonlight shimmers and shadows dance,
We twirl to the rhythm, caught in a trance.
Glass-like waters, a stage for our play,
In nature's comedy, we laugh all day.

Uncharted Thoughts in the Mist

Fog rolls in with a whimsical cheer,
Whispering secrets no one can hear.
Thoughts float like bubbles, popping in fun,
While clowns in the mist play tag with the sun.

The compass spins, lost in a game,
Leading us nowhere, yet all feels the same.
Ghost ships sail by, with laughter and jokes,
While mermaids giggle, playing hoax pokes.

Maps are for people too serious to roam,
We scribble our paths, wherever we comb.
Unlikely guides, the gulls lead the way,
With beaks full of breadcrumbs, they're ready to play.

Each step we take, more questions arise,
In the mist, we search for our biggest surprise.
Uncharted thoughts swell and begin to shout,
Lost but not lonely, that's what it's about.

The Call of the Distant Lighthouse

A lighthouse stands, with a wink and a grin,
While waves crash hard, determined to win.
It shouts, 'Ahoy!' to boats roaming free,
But everyone laughs—who's it calling? Not me!

Its light spins round, a disco of beams,
Searching for sailors, or lost in their dreams.
Rocks hide below, they chuckle and snort,
'They won't find us, they just miss the port!'

Seagulls dive down with their best feathered flair,
Mimicking dance moves as they soar through the air.
The keeper rolls his eyes, sips coffee with glee,
A show of absurdity that's plain to see.

So here we stand, on the shore of delight,
With echoes of laughter that stretch to the night.
In the arms of the waves, with all of our glee,
The call of the lighthouse—who needs to be free?

In the Embrace of Solitude

A crab danced by my flip-flop shoe,
It seemed to think we were a crew.
I tried to wave, it turned away,
So much for friendship on this day.

The seagulls squawk and steal my fries,
With sneaky moves and crafty eyes.
They laugh as I chase them down the shore,
Who knew my snack would spark a war?

Sunburned nose and sandy hair,
I wonder why I came out here.
With laughter ringing in the breeze,
Life's absurdity puts me at ease.

In solitude, my thoughts run wild,
Like a goofy and mischievous child.
The tide rolls in with a gentle shove,
And I embrace the silliness of love.

Harvesting Dreams from Dunes

I tried to build a castle grand,
But the waves had other plans at hand.
Sand sticks to me like playful grime,
As seagulls giggle—oh, what a crime!

The sunburnt man next to me snores,
While I'm waving to imaginary shores.
His straw hat flies off in the gust,
And I swear it has a life of its own, or bust!

With buckets and shovels, we dig for gold,
But just find seashells that smell like old.
We barter dreams with crabs in sight,
As laughter echoes into the night.

The moon rises high, a glowing face,
I dance with shadows, a goofy race.
With grains of dreams stuck on my palm,
Funnier still, it feels like balm.

The Symphony of Salty Air

The ocean sings a tune so bright,
But it's just the wind in a rambunctious fight.
I hear it calling, "Catch me if you can!"
And I'm flailing my arms like a poorly drawn man.

With each wave crashing, I feel like a clown,
My towel's a cape, I'm the king of this town.
I flip my hair like a dolphin retreat,
But only find seaweed stuck on my feet.

A pelican drops a fish with a plop,
And I gaze at the ocean, a hiccup, a stop.
In this festival of folly, I lose all my cares,
For even the gulls can't resist joining the flares.

As the sun sets, the dance reaches climax,
I trip on a flip-flop and roll down the backs.
Yet here, in this humorous, awkward sway,
Life's salty symphony leads the way.

Island Gestures of Time

The clock on the shore seems stuck in a spin,
Each second a wave, where do I begin?
It's frozen like jelly on a summer's eve,
While I'm in my sun hat, pretending to weave.

I take up a shell and hold it to my ear,
But it's just my mom's voice, quite loud and clear.
"Put on some sunscreen, don't fry like a crisp!"
And I chuckle, thinking of sun, tan, and lisp.

With time slipping by like sand through my toes,
I chase after sunsets, where the bright light glows.
I see shadows dance as day waves goodbye,
A wobbly ballet, oh my, oh my!

In this realm where moments seem to collide,
I wave to the past with an overly wide stride.
A playful gesture, something sublime,
For here, every heartbeat's a tick-tock of rhyme.

Dreams Cradled by Waves

As the sun dips low, the crabs start to dance,
A conch shell offers its best romance.
Flip-flops fly high, a seagull's new friend,
While fish in tuxedos swim fast with a bend.

A jellyfish giggles, floats by with a flare,
Says, 'In my glory, who needs a care?'
With each splashy wave, a secret is shared,
Life's a big joke, if only we dared.

From sandcastles high to the shoreline's own crease,
Starfish gossip, share their tales of peace.
But watch for those waves, they're cheeky and sly,
They laugh at our mishaps, oh me, oh my!

As the night unfolds, the moon's in a scene,
A party of dolphins, all dressed up and keen.
They flip and they twirl, under stars that glow bright,
A funny little ruckus, till morning's first light.

Tranquil Elegy at Dusk

The sun yawns wide, waves chuckle along,
Shells keep the rhythm, a bubbly song.
Fish in tuxedos with bow ties and tails,
Wave at the tourists, weaving their tales.

Laughter rises like bubbles in foam,
As crabs do the cha-cha, they're far from home.
With coconuts juggling, the parrots on cue,
They toast to the day, a coconut brew!

The canvas of twilight, painted in glee,
Boats rocking gently, a wobbly spree.
Seagulls complain of their lost shiny bait,
"Next time," they squawk, "we won't be so late!"

While shadows grow longer, the party ignites,
Starfish with sparkles, they dance into nights.
With each little giggle from waves at the shore,
Life on the water is never a bore!

Where the Sea Kisses the Sky

The horizon blushes with colors so bright,
Seagulls throw shade, it's a hilarious sight.
Sandbuckets topple, kids tumble and cry,
While crabs take a selfie, oh my, oh my!

Dolphins do flips, with grace and a grin,
"Life's just a ride, won't you hop in?"
With surfboards and giggles, the waves take a bow,
Who knew the sea had such fun here and now?

A kite in the sky takes a nosedive for fun,
As a kid on the shore turns and starts to run.
"Catch me, you kite!" he shouts to the sun,
But the sea just laughs, it has all the fun!

And when the moon rises, lighting the tide,
The shadows of fish can't help but collide.
A night full of chuckles, a splash at each swell,
Underneath the stars, all is peaceful and well.

Secrets Among the Coral

Under the waves, there's chatter galore,
Clams gossip secrets from their sandy floor.
The octopus winks, in its polka-dot suit,
While turtles debate, who'll win the pursuit.

Clownfish crack jokes, it's a comedy show,
As bubbles float up, in a jovial flow.
"Why did the grouper get locked out tonight?"
"It couldn't find a key, even with all its might!"

Sea urchins chuckle, their spikes in a knot,
"Just welcome the waves, give them all you've got!"
Rays glide in laughter, low in the blue,
Dancing with joy, just a wave or two.

And when evening comes, the spectacle's grand,
Starfish join in, forming a band.
Plucking at kelp, they serenade the shore,
With secretive grins, they can't help but roar!

The Sun's Reflection on Untamed Waters

In the mirror of the waves, I see,
A crab doing the cha-cha, wild and free.
The sun's warm grin on the fish's scales,
While seagulls squawk like they're telling tales.

Splashing waves tickle toes on the shore,
A sunburnt sailor yells, "One more!"
His hat flies off, a gull's tasty prize,
While the ocean rolls its joyful eyes.

Bubbles rise, they dance up high,
Like party balloons in a summer sky.
Dolphins leap, they steal the show,
As they twirl and twist in a watery glow.

A sunbeam's wink, the sea's bright laugh,
Makes even the fish look like they're taking a bath.
As laughter mingles with salt and spray,
We celebrate life in this silly ballet.

Requiem of the Drifting Leaves

Oh the leaves, they tango, swirling around,
Caught on a breeze, they're almost profound.
A leaf in a hat, a twig in a tutu,
Who knew that the forest had such a view?

With a rustle and shuffle, they dance on the floor,
An autumnal jamboree, who could ask for more?
One leaps atop puddles like it's ballet,
While another pretends it's a pirate at play.

Fallen leaves, they giggle and play tag,
While the wind, that mischievous old rag,
Tosses them high, like a game of charades,
Creating a symphony in lovely cascades.

So here's to those leaves, in their youthful spree,
Dancing their hearts out, wild and carefree.
In the quietest moments, they leave a mark,
As they giggle and flutter, alive in the park.

Labyrinths Carved by the Sea

The water weaves tales in sandy loops,
Where crabs and clams hold secret groups.
A labyrinth forms with each foamy crest,
As laughter erupts from the sun-soaked jest.

A starfish plays hide and seek with a shell,
While jellyfish float like they've drunk from a well.
The waves giggle softly, tickle the sand,
A game of hopscotch that's perfectly planned.

Tangled seaweed like hair in a mess,
Fish wearing hats could not be less.
We wander through twists, each turn a delight,
In this riddle of water, a glorious sight.

With every splash, the secrets unfold,
Their laughter to share, as stories are told.
Navigating through joy, we cheerfully roam,
In this silly maze, we've found our home.

Whispers of the Tide's Embrace

The tide whispers softly, a cheeky muse,
As sand tickles toes, you can't help but snooze.
An octopus waves with eight silly hands,
While seagulls drop treasures in shifty sands.

Buckets and spades, they declare the day,
Kids building castles in sandy ballet.
But oh! Here comes a wave with mischievous might,
It crashes down, turning sand into fright.

The foam frolics, a bubbly delight,
As laughter erupts in the warm morning light.
Starfish chuckle, they hug the rocks tight,
As the sea plays tricks, what a glorious sight!

So let's gather 'round where the sea meets the sky,
Where shadows of laughter dance and fly.
In the tide's gentle grasp, we find our place,
In the whirl of the ocean, we all find grace.

Dreams Cradled by the Sea

The fish wear hats and dance at night,
While crabs play chess, oh what a sight!
Seagulls shout jokes, with laughter so loud,
They form a band, drawing quite a crowd.

Turtles in shades ride waves with glee,
While dolphins juggle, splashing, carefree.
Mermaids sip coffee, writing their tunes,
As the sun yawns, painted by balloons.

Waves tickle toes, giggling at shore,
Sandcastles wobble, request encore!
The ocean's a circus, a vibrant spree,
Where even the coral pretends to be free.

So let your worries drift with the tide,
Join the sea's party, let joy be your guide!
For dreams are alive, where whimsy swells,
In this world where laughter always dwells.

Whispers of Forgotten Shores

A crab once lost his fancy shoe,
He asked some clams, but they just blew!
The wind laughed softly, tickled the sand,
As seaweed played drums, quite unplanned!

Stars peeked down, they twinkled in fun,
Like blinkers on taxis, they made a run.
A starfish stumbles, but don't you fret,
He waved a hello, with no regret!

Old boats gossip, wrapped in the mist,
They trade their tales, things you can't list.
Shells tell secrets, lost in the swell,
Of laughter so bright, it rings like a bell!

On these strange shores, where time takes a break,
Every wave whispers secrets to make.
So gather your joys, and toss in a cheer,
For the comical tides bring magic quite near.

Tranquil Horizons

With a wink from the sun, the day begins,
Fish wear tuxedos while doing the spins.
Gulls gossip loudly, about their last feast,
While the waves release laughter, a bubbling beast.

Shells have opinions, the crabs take a stand,
Arguing over who has the best sand.
The breeze throws a dance, swaying trees in tune,
While the coconut laughs, dropping a prune!

At dusk, the colors begin to swirl,
Horizons are painted, what a bright whirl!
The waves play tag, in a playful chase,
And the stars join in, in this cosmic race!

So stroll through this charm, where smiles are found,
In the rhythm of peace, your heart will abound.
For laughter's the language in this Eden's embrace,
Where every bit of joy finds its own space.

Mirage of the Distant Blue

A parrot practices stand-up on a tree,
With punchlines that make all the fish agree.
A turtle takes notes, with a thoughtful nod,
While sunbathers chuckle, lounging like a god.

Mirages of laughter float over the bay,
As octopuses juggle, just for play.
The beach is a stage, for whimsical plays,
Conducted by seaweed, in breezy ballet!

A swim in the blue holds tales untold,
Where mermaids tease dolphins, like pros of old.
Their giggles echo, rolling on by,
As they splash and tumble, 'neath the wide sky.

So dive into joy, splash in the fun,
For this distant blue warms everyone.
In the heart of the sea, where laughter runs free,
Is the magic of life, from sea to sea.

Tides of Thought

Waves crash like a tickled fool,
Thinking deep while on a stool.
Seagulls squawk a silly tune,
Dancing shadows 'neath the moon.

A crab with style scuttles by,
Winking at those who ask why.
Seaweed's hair in disarray,
It's having quite a lovely day.

I ponder life's sweet, salty fate,
With every splash, I contemplate.
Catch a fish, or catch a laugh,
The ocean's slapstick autograph.

As the tide begins to sway,
My worries wash away today.
Floating thoughts, so light and free,
Who knew sea air was so funny?

Echoes on the Shore

Footsteps dance on grains of gold,
Whispers from the waves unfold.
A jellyfish with a floppy hat,
Wobbles by, quite proud of that.

A sandcastle with a comical look,
Stands proud, like it's in a book.
Its turrets made from driftwood dreams,
Guarding secrets, or so it seems.

The tide calls out, a playful dare,
As seagulls laugh without a care.
Shells giggle as they roll along,
In salty air, they all belong.

Echoes of laughter fill the air,
With each splash, a silly flair.
Nature's humor, bright and bold,
In every wave, a story told.

Sanctuary in Solitude

On a rock, I sit and muse,
The ocean's scent, a funny ruse.
A starfish waves with all its might,
Doing yoga, what a sight!

Crabs in meetings, pinching paws,
Discussing life and its odd laws.
A lighthouse standing all alone,
Knows all secrets, like a phone.

With each wave, I chuckle low,
As fish parade in silly show.
Solitude is a joyous game,
In tranquil waters, I feel the same.

Nature's speech, a joyful tune,
Swaying under the watchful moon.
In this calm, I find delight,
Even the sea seems to be bright.

Beneath the Canopy of Waves

Bubbles rise with a giggle and pop,
Underwater, the silliness won't stop.
A sea turtle wearing shades,
Sipping tea as he parades.

Fish throw parties, fins a-sway,
"Come join us for a fish buffet!"
Coral reefs like confetti bright,
Dance to tunes of pure delight.

The octopus plays hide and seek,
Ink clouding, laughter at its peak.
Jellyfish in a wobbly show,
Float by, with a "Hey there, bro!"

Beneath the waves, where joy does bloom,
Echoes rise in a buoyant room.
Every splash is a dance, a cheer,
In the deep blue, laughter's near.

Odes to Solitary Shores

A crab with a hat, quite bold and bright,
Decides that the sun seems just right.
It dances away with a flick of its claw,
While seagulls just gawk, quite taken in awe.

The sand's a warm bed, for the clams to nap,
While shells tell stories, well that's a wrap!
But watch out for waves, they're sneaky and sly,
They'll drench your fancy flip-flops, oh why?

The sun sets down, painting skies with cheer,
As sandcastles crumble, it's plain to see here.
Let's laugh at the tides, that come and that go,
For they dance with a smile, as if in a show.

The laughter of fish, bubbles up from the deep,
While turtles are gossiping, secrets they keep.
In this watery theater, life's never dull,
Each wave tells a story, rich, bright, and full.

Currents of Nostalgia

Gather 'round folks, let's all reminisce,
Of times on the shore where we found our bliss.
With ice cream for dinner and sand in our toes,
Who needs a care? Just enjoy how it flows!

The sunburned nose that we used to wear,
And the funny way dolphins flew through the air.
Flip-flops went flying, oh what a sight,
As we chased after seagulls with all of our might.

Now every small wave sings a silly tune,
While fish joke about us—oh what a boon!
The old wooden pier creaks with glee and delight,
As it whispers our stories throughout the night.

So let's toast to laughter and memory's cheer,
With sand between toes and no worry or fear.
For time spent by water, oh how it delights,
Making each ordinary day feel just right.

Whispers of the Tides

The tides have a secret, or so they declare,
They whisper to crabs who wiggle and stare.
A rogue wave arrives, with a clap and a spray,
And uproots a fish who just wished to play.

Fluffy clouds float, like giant sea foam,
While seaweed's all tangled, a garden of home.
Oh, laughter erupts when a dolphin sneezes,
And fish roll around—nature's funny breezes.

Salty air tickles our noses so fine,
As we watch a starfish try on our shoes, divine!
With laughter and giggles, the sun starts to fade,
As crabs throw a party, with laughter displayed.

So here's to the waters, so witty and spry,
Where laughter's the current and humor's nearby.
The sea's enigmatic with tales that make sense,
Each splash tells a story, each wave a pretense.

Mirror in the Shoreline

Look closely, my friend, at the shoreline's face,
You'll see a reflection of giggles and grace.
A jellyfish wiggles, a curious dance,
While starfish conspire, plotting their chance.

Here comes a pelican, with a snazzy bowtie,
And a small hitchhiker who's ready to fly.
With every new tide, comes laughter anew,
While sand dollars whisper, "We read your review!"

The plucky old otter, a comedian true,
Cracks jokes at the barnacles stuck like glue.
"Why did the shell cross the beach?" he'd say,
"To get to the other side, what a day!"

So gather up shells, let's savor the sun,
For life at the shore just tickles our fun.
With mirrors in water that glimmer and shine,
Time spent by the waves is just so divine!

The Dance of Light on Water

The sun twirls on the waves,
Like a dancer in a bright dress.
Fish giggle as they play,
Making ripples, oh what a mess.

The seagulls join on the side,
Cawing jokes, quite absurd.
Splashing water, what a ride,
They dive down, their lines blurred.

A crab tries to join the fun,
But ends up tangled in seaweed.
Crab songs under the sun,
A chorus of laughter, guaranteed.

Each moment, a silly sight,
Nature's joy, a playful brawl.
With every splash, a delight,
In this watery carnival.

Remnants of Ancient Sailors

Old boots lie on the sand,
A testament to wild tales.
Perhaps they danced, hand in hand,
Or left behind, their fishy scales.

Sea chests filled with lost dreams,
Mysterious maps that were drawn.
Mermaids giggle at the schemes,
As they nibble on a prawns.

Ghosts of sailors sail by,
With a wink and a cheerful shout.
They whisper, 'Don't be shy!'
As they sashay and twirl about.

Polka dots and stripes collide,
On their pirate garb so bright.
Through the waves, they glide,
In a merry, winding flight.

Glistening Memories in the Foam

The foam frolics like a puppy,
Chasing the shore in a rush.
It bubbles up, feeling chubby,
Leaving behind a creamy hush.

Children laugh and run around,
Building castles, their hopes high.
"We are knights!" their chants resound,
As the waves wink and reply.

Old bottles float with a tale,
Drifting secrets with a splash.
They bob along, without fail,
Waiting for someone to dash.

Each crest holds a giggling past,
In the shimmer of the day's glow.
The memories fade so fast,
But their smiles continue to flow.

The Enchantment of Quiet Shores

The quiet shore whispers soft,
With shells that giggle and play.
A little turtle drifts aloft,
In search of snacks to sway.

Nearby, a parrot pretends,
To be a star of the scene.
Telling jokes that never ends,
In colors bright and green.

Each tide brings a wacky guest,
From crabs to the snorting seals.
They jest and tease, never pressed,
In nature's funny reels.

As sunset paints the sky with flair,
The shoreline dances at dusk.
With laughter filling the air,
While the stars begin to husk.

Hidden Treasures of the Deep

In the ocean's depths I seek,
A shoe, a spoon, perhaps some junk.
My treasure map? A doodle streak,
In crayon, the ink has shrunk.

A crab dressed up in pirate's gear,
Clangs his claws, 'You found my hoard!'
I apologize with a chuckle and cheer,
As he snatches my sandwich forward.

The fish parade in sequined scales,
They giggle as bubbles rise and pop.
It's all quite silly with their tales,
Of socks and hats that plummet, drop.

So here beneath an azure sky,
The laughter swims through seas of light.
With treasures that make a seagull sigh,
What a joy to stumble on this sight!

The Stillness Between the Waves

Where the water meets the sand,
A seal's attempting belly flop.
I can't quite gauge how well he'll land,
But the splash? A spectacular slop!

The gulls caw out, they mock his grace,
As he bounces in water, quite the scene.
I wonder if they have a race,
For clumsiness amongst the marine!

In the quiet, a treasure appears,
A toe, a bottle cap aglow.
Each grand find brings me to cheers,
A new collection of beachy show!

The sun dips low, casting fun shadows,
The breeze tells tales of splashes made.
In the stillness, oddities grow,
While laughter and waves dance in parade!

Mists of Belonging

In a fog that smells of fishy fries,
A mermaid spins her tales in jest.
Among the seaweed, oh what a surprise,
A clam that claims it's simply best!

I sit on rocks, pretending to think,
While friends nearby, they make quite the mess.
A sandcastle crumbles with each wink,
'Tis architecture at its best!

A dolphin passes with a wink,
He hints at secrets of the sea.
I wonder if he'd ever drink,
Fresh lemonade, just like me!

Amongst these mists, laughter thrives,
With treasures hidden in every swirl.
We chase the joy where fun arrives,
In waves that twirl like a lolling pearl!

Ripples of Reverie

The water winks with playful glee,
As I toss a pebble and watch it fly.
A circle forms, what will it be?
A fish that dreams or a seagull's sigh?

The tide takes time to tick and tock,
It skips like a kid who's lost his shoe.
While crabs play tag upon the rock,
And giggles echo, who knows what's true?

I found a bottle, it had a note,
"Help! I'm stuck under a boat!"
I laughed aloud, gave it my vote,
Should I rescue or just gloat?

As ripples dance and laughter twirls,
This sea of silliness surely swells.
A world of wonder, joy unfurls,
In this seaside tale that giggles and dwells!

Solitude Beneath the Palms

Sipping coconuts, feeling quite dull,
A crab scuttles by, with a furious pull.
I waved at a seagull, it just flew away,
Does it think I'm a beachcomber? I might just stay.

The sun is a furnace, my skin's feeling fried,
I asked for a drink, they handed me tides.
With each wave that crashes, my worries take flight,
But my hat nearly drowned, oh what a sight!

Palms sway above, whispering secrets so sweet,
Is the laughter from fish, or just my own beat?
The crabs hold their meetings, plotting their schemes,
While I fashion a throne from my soggy daydreams.

Alone but not lonely, a jest in the breeze,
A flip-flop's a throne if you sit with such ease.
With sand in my sandwich, the joy is a plus,
Each moment a treasure, just me and my rust.

Echoes of the Distant Horizon

I yelled at the ocean, it yelled back with glee,
Did we start a contest? It's hard to foresee.
The waves chuckle softly, a bubbly refrain,
As I slip in the surf, and lose half my brain.

A dolphin is laughing, or maybe it's me,
With seaweed as my crown, I dance wild and free.
The sun beams above, a spotlight on my dance,
While seagulls critique my ungraceful prance.

From a palm tree I hear a reluctant applause,
The wind adds a rhythm, with no need for cause.
I twirled with a shell, but it clanged like a pot,
With echoes of laughter, I wedged 'tween the lot.

The horizon is distant, yet feels so well near,
With bubbles of fun, I could drown in the cheer.
Should I write them a letter? A postcard on foam?
Or just laugh at the tide, my floaty home.

Serene Shores of Memory

The waves tell a tale, of days gone by,
Of sandcastles crumbled, oh my oh my!
I tried to build high, but the tides were unkind,
And now I sit here, with a shell on my mind.

A mermaid strolled past, with a wink and a wave,
I offered my snacks, she was suddenly brave.
We plotted new ways to snag fish and more,
But a clam at my feet laughed till it was sore.

The sun started setting, the colors like fire,
I thought of my worries, and tossed them on hire.
The gulls formed a band, with their squawks as the tune,
While my laughter bubbles up, mixing with the moon.

In these serene echoes, my thoughts laugh and play,
The memory's a blanket, all cozy and gray.
So I'll stick to this joy, like glue to a shell,
And remember my summer, quite oddly, quite well.

Shadows on the Water

The fish all conspire, with whispers so sly,
Swapping my snacks for a wave and a sigh.
I scribble confessions, on the sand, oh so fine,
Only to watch them dissolve—what's that? A sign?

The sun paints a canvas with colors so bright,
I ask for a portrait, the breeze gives a fright.
My shadow stretches long, like a giant banana,
While I trip over flip-flops, my own little drama.

The moon starts to giggle, throwing silver around,
As shells hold their breath, without making a sound.
I chase after ripples, feeling quite spry,
But the tide pulls me back like a sneaky old guy.

In shadows that dance, a parade seems to form,
With laughter erupting, keeping spirits warm.
Though the water may quench, my thirst for pure fun,
With joy in each splash, my day's just begun!

www.ingramcontent.com/pod-product-compliance
Lightning Source LLC
Chambersburg PA
CBHW072126070526
44585CB00016B/1558